African Spring

First published by Staging Post in 2018

10 Orange Street
Sunnyside
Auckland Park 2092
South Africa
+2711 628 3200
www.stagingpost.co.za

ISBN 978-1-928440-01-7

Cover design by Palesa Motsomi
Creative direction by Karabo Phogole
Sounding board: Letuka Dlamini
Leaf design by Harryarts - Freepik.com
Editing by Megan Mance
Proofreading by Linda Da Nova
Set in Minion Pro 10/14pt
Printed by CTP Printers, Cape Town
Job no. 003345

African Spring

POEMS

Uhlamurile Mabunda

To my mother, for raising two bad kids (mostly) on your own. To my late father and elder brother, you guys hurt me when you left and I'm still mad but I know you still look down and guide me when I need you. To my younger brother for testing my patience and my grandmother for being an absolute G of a matriarch. This is also for my friends who recognised my words as more than just scribbles.

The careful impartation of wisdom among
generations is a gift that nurtures greatness.

Prologue

Your telepathic gaze and unflinching conviction to the revolution
Taught us how to escape the rainbow's colourful gifts and illusions
You conquered being alone and remained the nation's only stone
As they tried to feed us a lukewarm version of your fire
Hoping it does not boil inside us and inspire us to enquire

Freed you from the cells and failed to imprison you in their state
Branded the bandit of Brandfort, severed your voice from our hearts
Left us to whisper your name while they scolded us with their cold guns
Pouring blood on your name and telling us we cannot be your sons
Starved us of our mother using distance to step on your tongue
Lest we learn to speak of the season when Africa has its spring

Wearing robes, baring teeth and sold your life for a loaf of bread
In the name of a deity that they were rather ready to offer your head
They come now that you are gone and sing your praises instead
Not knowing your silence nurtured the garden of defiance
Using the rain as a compass and our signal not to act on impulse

The heavens wept as we planted your seed in the ground
Now that we know you will grow from it, we will fight for this land
We will tend to your garden and lend our people a hand

Mama Nomzamo Winifred Zanyiwe Madikizela-Mandela

Thank you

Contents

Philogyny

(n) the love or deep admiration for women.

BookOne

"
we need to respect and love our women
wholeheartedly
"

Heart of a Matriarch

I took my time to let an old woman talk
Only twenty-one, I said teach me how to walk
I'll bargain for your words, get a building block
Never seen her in tears, joy the greatest shock
She said sit down son, let me teach you how to rock.

Pay a little attention, instruction of importance
Treat your wife well, with utmost reverence
Be your own man, define independence
Converse with God, get repentance
Forget this not, your point of reference.

Keep you safe, make some choices
Yes against you there will be voices
Soft spoken making loud noises
I bless you now, give you providence
Live by the truth, have a heart that rejoices.

Now, I'm 83 and I've given life all of me.

Thou Art Man

It aches to be equated to men that beat women and spoil their hair
The same women who will not dare deny their bloodline an heir
To call out *uncle* to a being that led my sister to lay bare in his lair
And watch my aunt shed tears while keeping the evil in her
prayers
We have been quiet about this but have we not seen our biggest
fears?

Madness and awful verity when there aren't enough men left to
be Men
There are men-shaped carcasses parading in the glory of a time
when
Men had no urge to violate their own daughters and tear their
hymen
Girls were in no hurry to be grown and exhibit qualities of women
Women walked with heads high for they knew they were equal
human

But now they don't woman enough when judged by how best they
can man
Untaught that their part and purpose was created with man in
tandem
Attend to her wound before there is not enough left of her to be
Woman
For the mountain and I can only tell a king when it's time to lead
his clan
But only a woman that respects your affection will declare you a
man.

A Simple Man

Let me remember to be the man I was raised to be, never satisfied
with dreams I can simply see
I pictured you joyful from the little I had to give, a magnified
sensation that's another reason to live
Share a life with you that's lavish in currency that feeds the soul
more than it requires a man to toil
Let me share my vision with you so you can influence my
provision, yet I am just a man

Let my arms be the safest place you ever hold on to and my mind
the warmest place you ever enter
I'll sleep closest to the door and open it every morning when your
feet hit the floor and you prepare to roar
Let me share any wrong that burdens you, and I'll surely protect
the destiny that awaits you
I can't always understand your bruises, I'll respect the walk of fire
your ego chooses, yet I am just a man

Let me be there to teach you how to hold a paintbrush and adjust
your wrist and ball a fist
To understand that every stroke of your voice paints me a picture
of a future secured in hope
That true strength understands the value of weakness, to carry
calm even at your angriest
Let the words I utter to you be registered as spoken art to your
heart, yet I am just a man

I pray you let me lead you in prayer, that I help you up when it
hurts me to stand on this foyer

Littered with error, my path was not a mistake, strange to you
    because it was not yours to take
The only sort of friendship I understand is one that endures
    hardships and trials withstands
You walk confidently by yourself less any much need, know that I
    will lead, yet I am just a man

The heart matters, not too long ago mine was in tatters but that's
    nothing that flatters
A result of promises that turned to dust and sportingly I've tried
    to create love from lust
I've never understood its verbal meaning but I have always shown
    a little more than feelings
I know my purpose and what's at stake and I will give you a part
    of me that only you could break
I fall in love with life and drift besides myself every time I see a
    black woman being her queenly self
Her majesty yearns for my kingly affection, steps of royalty are my
    motivation, yet I am just a man

You are oblivious to my dreams and I'm aloof to my past, yet I am
    here to show you a man at last
I'm standing here at the door to eternity, seeking a life lived
    abundantly seasoned righteously
I put forth daily an honest representation of everything I have
    been taught to be, so look carefully

I am just a simple man.

Tree of Arcs

I am a patriarch raised by a matriarch, my graceful leader
Having savoured prose, I resolved to measure patriarchy
As never mutually exclusive, for one breeds the other
And probed the standing all in the midst of anarchy

Mentally elevated to guard the life-giving force of femininity
Where clans are moulded and modelled on a layer of arches
Explored the raw emotion that fuels the fire in masculinity
But never has such splendour emanated from a lone monarchy

Where our differences overflow within us, intended to be shared
Disdainfully we spurned the ideology prescribed by biology
And what we lack is consummated with souls enmeshed
Have we sold the will to give of ourselves to feed the tree?
Perplexing one another, we cultivate family roots disengaged
Paraded as equality we strip our temples of birthing capacity

The story perpetuated is we cannot prevail in symmetry
But whatsoever -archy leads, the other empowers by proxy

Cry My Son

My son, from the day you are given life by your mother's womb
Cry my son, until the day your children carry you to your tomb
Howl and hold not back the tears that poison your kindness, man
Wail your pain out as a child so it does not possess you as a man.

Dear son, you first will nurse the heart of the one who lets you in
Whose first instruction to your daughter is to protect against your
    kin
An echoing of the scars of a failed generation by those in your
    skin.

Listen my son, be man enough to understand the words I speak
Show strength to a society that will call you weak when your eyes
    leak
Let your tears wet the ground and water the seeds of the world
    you seek
Then and only then will your heart let your spirit learn to speak.

Hear me my son, do not harden your soul for the sins of your
    father.

Once a Child

I've been to the edge of every cliff
You do not need to speak of yourself
It was not your place to teach me to be a man
But, hear me speak, because I know a woman

I was her first and she held me without a clue
Despised the things I sometimes put her through
Painfully controlling my desire to be wild
Unquestionably, it hurt her more to use the rod

I asked the questions and she found the answers
Even when I had run out of second chances
I wonder if it makes her smile to think of me
Questioning if I've became the man she hoped I'd be

I pray you look at your son now and see a man
You carried me; you are more than just a woman

My Brother's Keeper

I was a coward when I turned predator to your cries
And saw you with that mini above your knees so high
Looked at your body like Kentucky fried thighs
Undressing you in my head while you spoke over slides
And the lunchtime remarks about your ass being nice

Yes I was a coward when I minded my own business
Knowing your screams at night gave birth to bruises
My friend is impotent but you're the one he abuses
Claiming a barren woman is to him of no significance
When he is the one with tools that cannot reproduce?

I was a coward when I let you fall prey to the unjust
Failed to protect you against my father staring at your bust
Who offered you drinks to fuel his desire and filthy lust
Knowing his price will be paid in full with every thrust
While he divides your milkshake so his pipe don't rust

I was a colossal coward when I let my brother say I do
Knowing of all he really does when he is far from you
Playing daddy to offspring he fathers without you
With a woman that only just found out about you
Unable to handle this being her baby number two

As a common curtesy to the generations that come after me
Let me speak for the ranks of boys and men alike in our times
We have fumbled and failed dismally in addressing our crimes
Daughters of the soil, please forgive me in all my forms
I am my brother's keeper and all his errors are my wrongs

Negrophilia

(n) an affection for, or interest in the black race.

Book Two

"
so that we unite and collectively
take back our power as a people
"

Show Them Everything

They can see you fall
And they may see you crawl
Maybe even lean up against a wall
But don't ever let them see you cry

Let them see you bleed
Or break sweats as you breathe
Or even beg if you have to plead
But don't ever let them see you cry

Sure, they can choose to mock you
Or hurt their chest while laughing at you
Sometimes even place judgement upon you
But don't ever let them see you cry

Release them to frame your scars
Or give you fame as you pass
By describing your days as a farce
But don't ever let them see you cry

When it ends and it's all over
They will look at you and ponder
What exactly makes you smile better?
So, don't ever let them see you cry

They may catch you as you fall to a knee
And yet a lot of them really aren't free
Show them everything they want to see
But don't ever let them see you cry

Little Jimmy

Little Jimmy, a dreamer born in a place that's not his home
His ancestry yonder far from the land he thinks he owns
Chased education for corporates to read his credentials like he
fumbled
Hereditarily travelling twice the distance contending for half the
reward
Patronising drivers double locked their doors as his stomach
rumbled

Raped by the prospect of opportunity laced with rejection
for him to mount
His humanity is valued and often fluctuates with his bank account
Stripped of all he owned and bled to reclaim it, what he recovered
is scant

Woke up swimming in sweat, drenched in fear
Screaming, howling, Mommy I had a nightmare
The type of which to any being would be hard to bare

His mother sighed and wept as he retold his fantasy
She was certain that this was already a black child's reality
For theirs a human spirit, forged in strength to thrive immortally

Liquorice

I carry the black wherever I go, given a moment to be coal, I may touch you and leave a smudge. Then show me a righteous man and I'll tell you the lies that made him honest, or point to a white man that thinks him heartless. This might leave a lingering relish in your views, the smell of charred humanity is all I see on your face when you regard me, this is bound to be the story when the sun is out and your shadow all has the glory, filled with compassion, I offer my hand to help you up, for responsibility will always overshadow popularity.

From the blackness of my iris I look at a woman and perceive a queen, the telling sight of greatness engraved in darkness. See she carries a viscous soul, pliable in appearance but resilient in attendance, yet undemanding enough to flow through the heart and veins of the man she calls her king, she is that Nubian goddess crafted in an ebony furnace, that queen of Sheba bathed in milk and honey, scented in wisdom, her black skin burns from her spirit within, don't ask her to be light, panthers always walk upright, take time to learn to love her the way she likes to be loved, with the deepest darkest passion, that will sparkle just like marble.

Charcoal in complexion, I am not the symbol of your "free" but embody everything that you fear. I mean it has got to be more than the colour of your mould, more to do with the flavour of your soul and even the story of your lineage that was told. If you have a midnight heart, the blind will see clearly because hate is colourless in the mind. My colour is primary and presumably offensive but much to my disbelief, the disruption of my ties seems just right for you to line your greed parading in collars seeming white, you look at me with disgust and wonder if you will ever earn my trust?

I was born a king, raised a prince, walked on hot stones and grew a tough skin, so you may ask what type of royalty has a tongue so crude, unrefined and yet so principled? Velvet utterances can sometimes be rude, but see there is *authentic* in his walk and energy in his talk, it has been recorded that you covet the culture he oozes but lack the courage to use it, history will look at me and see a man defined by respect and not defiled by contempt, I dip myself in tar so despite my walk to uhuru being far, I see you still wonder if my skin tastes like liquorice.

Uhlamurile Mabunda

Hi Lava Msava

Hi lava msava!

Let us be clear, we are not here to negotiate
Or offer a path to which you may affiliate
In fact, we do not require that you assimilate
The ground beneath you insists that you vacate!

Si funa umhlaba!

If your vessels came to shore laden with land from over the sea
Go, head back and carry with you what you say you did not steal
You sunbathe and beg for my pigmentation, instead you peel
Your presence is a disturbance even the spirits can feel

Re batla lefatshe!

The drum will sound, hearts will pound, and tears fall to ground
The African spirit, proud and loud will not be owned
Its purpose is often inhibited but never to be dethroned
The day will come, do not be wanting when you're found

Ri khou ṭoda lefhasi!

Audacity

The persistence of the Caucasus' descendants incessantly insistent
on justice when he feels victim to a crime he was previously
acquitted of?

Like lines of mercy faded and hidden by heresy used to conceal a
bloodline of witchery disguised as clergy trading smiles with
the enemy.

And the ungrateful guests that turned our gardens into pits of
cess

Watered with the blood of ours while they take turns to play chess.

When truth comes to light and you see the darker shade of white
claiming to do only what they deem right in their sight?

The caucacity!

Riding on the Sun

Take a ride to the sun on empty purses full of purpose
Cultivating desire to compose and sign your corpus
Hitchhiking on the shadow of the vision it chases
Feeding that raging fire screaming from your soul
As the moon sweats from that stolen gold it holds
Never lose sleep dreaming of days you can slumber
Anything but this moment is a life lived in sombre
Colonise your heart, while its fears are plundered
You may burn, but ride the sun in all its wonder
So you see your idea of comfort bleeding ember.

Atonement

Who told you tales about their discovering and exploring, when
 it's really just appropriating?
The stories that are a citation that dead men can't speak and no
 matter what truth you seek
The victor will inscribe his story and write that as what will come
 to be known as your history
Lace it with ego and noble intentions and paint it with laughs
 because lies are infectious
Trying to call the richness of your dark skin ugly while they
 continue with its smuggling

The centre is where the concentration of melanin is darkest and
 Africa is wealthiest
Where the sun was born and still returns every morning to have
 breakfast with relatives
And they wonder what still attracts the sun to this land after they
 looted and plundered it?
Questioning what we buried so deep within our land the sun
 keeps coming back home?
Why it comes to colour us black and extricate us from their
 loathing even to our bones?

Because you are forged of the same fire that keeps the sun alive
 and burning over hot stones
Your likeness is divine and often they try to loan and pinch but
 can never adequately clone
Black child listen to that voice telling you to do it when you stare
 in awe of your golden throne
You are beautiful in your multitudes of tones and every morning
 embrace from the sun atones

Captive

How you define freedom
Determines what you are free from
When held captive by your own wisdom

Nothing Shorter

You will say my name right! Even if it takes you 'til time is night
You will round the vowels and assert the consonants
You will narrate my title and use it to summon constellations
I cannot allow your fallacy to bestow a nickname upon me
My ancestors do not know the insult with which you wish to call
    me
I require that you say my name, you will sound it on the hills and
    recite it like poetry
And until you command every syllable, every letter, your tongue
    will burn with eternal envy
While you sulk that there's nothing shorter, repetition of my name
    will be your only commentary

Ubuntu

(n) a quality that embodies humanity and compassion.

BookThree

"

and formulate thoughts that lead
us to a better sense of self

"

Obsessed with Perfection

Pastor pardon what I preach, I protest to perform for your praise
Pause and ponder why I picket to propagate a phenomenal
    presence
Prognosis of my paradox bares proximity to my panoramic past
Place my head on a pillow and pray I remain unpunished by
    poverty

Prepared a pact not to paint a pity picture with a piano
Paralysis of my purse fails to prohibit God's plan for my plenty
Placid palindromes of character propel my passion for a level of
    parity
Peace being persuasion, I do not prostitute principles for a
    premium

People profess and paraphrase what is poor and punitive
Palpitations beyond pheromones planted by a patient partner's
    purpose
Pursue a pragmatic path leading to a pleasing promise for a purist
Pride pollutes my presentation, permit it not to poison persona

Purchased a pair and polished my prospect of the positive
Profit of pretence is a parade of pain in the palace of a plodder
Parallax of power can parch, possess and pacify your pulse
Perhaps I'll play a profound portrayal of pretty on the podium

Perception of perfection is imperfect, I am a perfect imperfection

Camouflage Lies

Up at three am and my head bleeds thoughts,
The same thoughts I thought would have been well thought
throughout the subconscious thought stream called dreams,
The same thoughts that ought to be brought down like inheritance
to elevate my stature it seems,
The same thoughts that hunt the time I thought I owned sought
with eyes that resemble nothing less of greed, like a bad seed
my heart grieves.

Flattery of imaginary efforts has me wondering whether the line
of things not done and things that have been done can set
apart what has to be done from all that cannot be done, doing
the doable and undoing the unjustly done, in order to do right
by so doing, and all that does this is a desire dismissed as a
dream?

Who is reality to tell me that the focus is flawed and cannot
be followed? For that flaw-filled file fuels the fountain of
favourable fantasies flowing through the funnels of freedom.

But after all, it was just a dream, right? Or just lies that make the
night seem right.

Untold

I have much respect for wise people, even when they grow old
I have made the decision to be that man, though I may seem cold
I take time to listen, even though I don't always do as I'm told

I make time to study life, I may fall and fail but I'll never fold
I make sacrifices today, I hope my tomorrow is blessed a thousand
    fold
I am gonna be brave, clad in all gold become my family's
    stronghold

I took the road less travelled, foolish I got labelled but really, I
    was bold
I took time to love without lust, a home is not merely a household
I know you'll look back at the life I live and this true story will
    be told

I Never Left You

I betrayed you, I battered you
I commanded you to hush when you lent me wisdom
I kicked you in the teeth, when you let slip the truth

I insulted your comprehension and subjected you to lustful
    seasons
I evoked emotions and tabled a motion to sensor your devotion
I used my pride to numb your speech and continue with the
    senseless

I let the sun shine on my pain after the rain washed my tears
I prostituted my loyalty to be servant only to the moment
I crushed the consequences of compromise and made sacrifice
    my concubine

My conscience, I beseech you, can I be yours again?
A voice in my head said "you have always been".

Full of It

It's those deceitful that leave you tearful
If you are mindful it might make you thankful
If you are spiteful it could leave you shameful
It's a little awful that makes way for a lot of grateful

When you are youthful you are not always tasteful
Sometimes the cheerful leaves you colourful
Looking zestful and all you really are is wishful
Leaving you fearful while looking to be successful

I appreciate an elderly earful it's always useful
It's the heavy and the truthful that I find helpful

If I remain faithful and careful, life can be wonderful

The Paradox of Proposition

Can I gain without pain, does it have to be a strain?
Carefully follow, you'll question if purpose can be so plain
And the most beautiful sunshine be daughter to the rain

Trying gives birth to failure when success is the desired destination of rest
But failing to try will impress when your goal is an achievement without a test
Dreams that live to see their death are clothed in fear and claim to be the best
Often reincarnated to haunt a sunlight it never saw, though only the brave attest

I cannot exclude disclosure of the simple when handling complicated treasure
The panic I had, harboured a measure of hope and was breeding composure
The ugly sacrifice is never painted with the beauty of leisure but abundant in pressure
As apologetic as my pride may be, I will always have humility at the sight of pleasure

I Saw It All

Set against a backdrop of black business
Where broad-based is a bureaucrat's bus to bulging bags
A bewildering brotherhood to an observant bystander
Where blows and bastings are the basis for a tender bliss,
                                        I saw a fist fight today

On the ever-evasive embodiment of eclectic egos
Where education is expected exclusive to the elite
And ethnic eloquence is exclaimed as exotic
It is ethical to eavesdrop on economic envoys because,
                                        I saw a fist fight today

Along the alleyways of an ancient Azania
An abandoned way is assigned to the archives
Of alien aristocrats, averse to African association
Yet their armies arrest any attempt to air our achievements yes,
                                        I saw a fist fight today

Cocooning in the corridors of corporates
Where cubicles incubate concubines
Conniving to conceive heirs of currency
And cloaks and daggers are a career's curse dammit,
                              I saw a fist fight today

On the hollow heartstrings of hostile hoaxes
Here, a hungry hunk hustling for a holla haphazardly
Hunting a healing honey hurting for her husband
Hoping he holds her hand habitually heading for heaven oh,
                              I saw a fist fight today

Erupt when majestic manumit melanin mauled malevolence
And maverick multitudes manifested a marvellous mutiny
Match lit to mortify the moot manipulative minions
Now malleable in this magnificent moment of madness
                    Make no mistake, I saw it all today

Dear Self

I couldn't get through this change unscathed
Or walk through the exorcism unchanged
Finding words to explain why it didn't last
Or fumbling to explain why I let me trust

Tried to abscond and run as far as I could outwards
Saw peace of mind had listing yet none for cowards
Treaded a path that was bound to lead me away
Seems thoughtless to say that there I did not stay

I came back with a bloody portrait of happy
A beautiful visual of how life can be candy
A sweet taste of humble when I was at my worst
Dear Self, Remember to always put You first

Social Convention

Pretty little liars we've turned out to be
Posting pictures living so carefree
Thinking this will make you like me
Is it so painful not to pretend?
Are we hurtful just so we trend?
Serving you depictions of fictitious tea
Often crying at the lies I make you see
Even I wonder what it's really like to be me.

Internal Affairs

I had a moment and that's that
The conscience or the heart, yes it was about that
I said to myself I'm going to write about that
And at that instant I thought now how about that?

Then I realised that there is more to it than meets the eye
Because a decision made for one means the other has got to cry
Friends they cannot be despite all the efforts they try
I must confess that even today I have no answer as to why
Surely this cannot be all that I'm called to live by?
I don't want to question my purpose way after I die.

In the present war to become conscious
I enslave my life to the laws of my conscience
And my heart cannot be trusted or so says my sub-conscience
So, I try believing my head even if it's just a convenient coincidence.

Yet acting as my lawyer the heart says
Your happiness is every reason behind my ways
You follow this cold calculated conscience like religion for days
But you never see the wages it always says it pays.

How long will it be before your conscience betrays you?
How long will it be before it collects the bounty on you?
Haven't you always felt all that I've offered to you?
I didn't want it to come to this but without me, it'll be the end of
    you.

The conscience smiles and says: You are because I existed
Not because I want you restricted
But to keep your desires convicted
And give you a platform to show just how you are gifted
The irony is that the cause of our differences is to see you lifted
And in all the feuds the focus has not been shifted.

My monologue had made me question my sanity
I was thrown back to reality and survived all that controversy
And because my kindness is measured by my cruelty to those that
    bring forth loyalty
I cannot be separated from adversity.

Circle of Light

Is the sun kind or the moon blind?
Every morning I watch the sun rise to heal with warmth
A world that was cold to the moon, but will be cruel 'til noon
until it vanishes into the skyline when the moon feels safe again to
    return in the evening.

Who is chasing who?

Forever stuck inheriting a land that pretends to love you when
    you shine but covets another when you turn your spine.

Who betrays who?

The Old Guard

Derived from chronological divide, differences have spawned a psychological bind and have the mind believe it is free, though entangled in bouts of the precedent, yet the mental trap you fall into is all too evident.

Your choices are limited to what has been predefined and still you call it freedom all for the sake of being a part of this kingdom? Is this the same freedom that has become a victim of euphemism because we preach diversity but think in controversy?

Let's challenge the superiority in seniority because it seems a farce in my eyes to have security in similarity!

Love

*(n) a strong and passionate feeling of
deep affection for another person.*

BookFour

"

actively nurture and grow fruitful
and loving relationships

"

Cappuccino with Cream

Filled to the brim with a fluffy cream
it tastes like we were once a team
a hot beverage erupting liquid dreams
the lovely mess of beautiful swirling steams
as it seems, timeless is the time we spent
I stayed drunk off the caffeine and your scent
sober now to write these words and be honest
it still stings like I'm sleeping with hornets

listen, my presence was decent to you
and you were somewhat perfect for me
but we, we were never really good for us
broken legs couldn't stop us, if anything but
I would close my eyes and fall into your trust
our souls mingled long before we went bust
smiling joyfully while courting wanderlust
holding you close again, if I could just …

you made me feel good with just a sip
and hypnosis when you swayed your hips
with emotions you sprinkled on your lips
I love that the angel in you still makes me skip

Untitled Love

I wonder if the object of my affection
could only be a figment of my imagination.
What it is I love about you is unknown
but you make me feel things I've never known.

Your presence in my heart causes sleepless nights,
thoughts of you shower my heart in lights.
The heart believes it's real and tries to make you stay,
just when I thought there was more to see, you fade away.
Your smile has been engraved on my distant gaze,
since I last saw you, it has only been days.

Heart pounds like you are getting close to me
but with my naked eyes nothing is all I see.
Daydreaming about you is never a moment wasted,
oh, how I wish you existed.

Just Remember This

Joy has a way of making it all seem okay
Coy as it may be, makes my fears feel okay
Once I tried to cry while I was hurting for you
Surely now I smile because once, I had all of you

Thoughts said it would be hard without you here
Played your part, flipped the script and left me there
Pretty little bumblebee, I picked you out the hive
Funny how all this is a colourful part of the archive

I remember I sat and in my head, made you my wife
Today I smiled and simply wished you a better life
The stage was set, we lit up yeah, I did us right
Curtains fell and I gave applause, I did not fight

I dare you to let it be, be still and let me leave
I care more than you'll ever see, a new life I'll let you live

It's All About Her

Listen while I talk about her, you might have seen her and maybe
even met her
She makes an occasion and dresses in designer garments, just to
go to the mini-market
She has her accounts in order, the sense in her head – would
mean little if she only had notes in the bank

Listen while I talk about her, she might love this and tell you
about her
Not only vocal, she has a voice to speak to a hardened heart and
softly make it heard
Not only sexy, she has the body to give birth to an entire nation
and all she wants is adoration
Not only fragile, she carries the world but will only cry on a
shoulder

Listen while I talk about her, she might be kind to you and let you
be there
I'm talking about that girl who questions my actions and plans
my motives
I'm talking about that lady who offers her bosom when I'm weak
and embraces me while I speak
I'm talking about that woman who calls me her man, because her
dream was not perfect

Listen when I talk about her

Come with Me

He was a wordsmith of a sweeter reality crafted in careful
    conversation
She was a traveller from a broken land in pursuit of her perfection
They were clothed in pasts stained in a similar discolouration

She said please sit with me tonight and they got acquainted
He said let's have a little colour and a simple picture he painted
They were drawn as neighbours to good places, where they felt
    appreciated

She popped her eyes out and marvelled with ecstasy at his
    anomaly
He kept her presence, impressed by her character quite easily
The ground they walked on massaged their feet quite comfortably

He had a fiery rich caramel treat that demanded his affection
She preferred a hard dark chocolate that melted to her attention
They indulged in dessert and tasted mindless intoxication

She wanted the space, she felt safe beyond the box that was formed
He extinguished her worry and a perfect bond was fashioned
They established that things that are good for you are never forced

He was simple minded as she was minded wisely
They were on an eternal path to happy

Friend Zone

Open letter to sister girl, do not burden me with your lust
I have my own to struggle with, don't blind me with your bust
Eyes gaze at me with suspect desire, let me get this off my chest

Adjust the way you look at me, I see a friendship in our ties
We've only just met, show me your heart and not your thighs
Put your integrity forward before we converse, forget the lies

I'd like to equate yokes before we compare notes, to be understood
Let's connect deeply and have you keep your dignity like you
    should
Please tell her we can only be friends, I'm sorry if she
    misunderstood

My Walk with Love

If I had a little to say, my lips would ask your soul if I could touch
you
And with something to say, I would remind you of the beauty in
you
All we need is a friend but there are roles only lovers can play
While watching the sunset there are words only brothers can say
Let me remind you that I have been listening to your heart today
And saw the fire in your eyes expectant of affection all day
I suppose it's okay to walk out from a past that tried to have me
slain
Healing has me crazy and smiling facing what used to be my pain
I guess I needed some time to make sense of it all before my
comfort
Feeling always took over reason and caused a mess without any
effort
It is only right I acknowledge the lessons I was quick to judge as
fault
The song in my head assures me that I have your support
I need you by my side if I am going to survive my walk in this land
I don't have much to say to you but let me take your hand

Bliss

So ... listen to this,
I met this miss with a sultry smile that spoke with a lisp
walked with a sensual sway in her hips,
my spirit was snatched and ready to fight and call dibs,
I mean she was a tall, melanoid glass and I wanted to take every
    sip,
with her brown skin glowing in the sun and still being kissed,
only a saintly voice could come from her African lips,
the moment she said hi my heart was pleased and did some flips.
Yo, she was waisted like a wasp, every breath I took was my last
    gasp,
and the afro she donned was the stuff that other kids wish,
even as I watched her eat I thought to myself what a yesses!
I imagined I held her hand and went on trips,
for this kind of happiness there wasn't even a script,
she was brown and her soul so bliss,
I was a mess.

Excuse Me Miss

I remember meeting you as a stranger; you looked at me and wore
your smile so gently
I get happy when you understand my kind of stupid and speak of
it so eloquently
It's my jealousy that won't understand why you tweet before you
share your story
You could even catch me staring; amazed by every imperfection
that makes you pretty
I may even lie awake sometimes in fear so I never have to wake
up to your vacancy
But I will always share with you what I feel, even if the sentiments
are not so fancy

It hurts to feel that it can heal wounds it's been known to cause,
is it really Love?
That the death of the guilt it kills lays a seed of innocence that the
loveless Crave
Riddled that it makes you happy whether you give it or receive it;
it can only be Love
And if I had it unconditionally, I would continue to breed it by
how I would behave
I was raised to treat the recipients of mine with reverence, betray
not the one I have
And if my actions don't speak love to you, then surely my
intentions cannot be of Love
You have granted me refuge in your space for some time and I
really have to say that I have grown to appreciate this place,
so let me slow down with the poetry and convey a little reality,

I saw you once covered in white and I thought I just might watch
you take flight,

but I wasn't sure so I took you on a tour, carefully observing
how you planted your steps as you walked and watered your
tongue before you spoke,

listen, it was the humility in your smile that said I should, but
your eyes, your big eyes considering new beginnings showed
me that I could,

and I'll confess what I saw was already blinding to my youthfulness,
so I closed my eyes and solicited a divine conversation and
even that was filled with hope that was binding to my silence.

My honour said it needed to be true if I was to do it, so I got you
roses.

Do Speak Ill of Me

Allow me to speak out of turn and impose on you words along
these lines

I hope you highlight all my rough edges, someone might just
know how to polish them to an acceptable shine

Remind your heart to tell them how I broke the only part of you
I never really had

How I cared least about what you were really there for and said
some stuff that probably got you mad

I liked it because I knew that you would grow to hate that you
loved just how it was flexible

You bred resentment when I resisted, because I understood
exactly why you persisted way past sensible

Be sure to mention how I made you cry but to speak of it would
have me ask you why

I hope it is spoken of how I did not understand what you were
saying when you looked at me with watery eyes

And tell them that in all reality I could not claim to be a stranger
to walking away

Surely the cause was my presence because in essence it made you
want to believe I would find a way to stay

Strange feeling when I found my head having conversations
about your likeness
I wouldn't dare say I almost missed you because it wouldn't quite
resemble the me you know to be heartless
I remember asking you to pick your favourite colour so you could
leave your mark
A pretty elaborate colour scheme when you painted over my
barriers so you could feel at home in the dark
I am not proud that I was always honest with you and not always
real with myself
But I looked in the mirror once, I gave me that look of how I
needed time to be put on the shelf

So please do speak ill of me, the ugly truth behind why I am not
by your side
As a notice to those who might know a little more of me, so my
narcissism has nowhere to hide
I pray you are sincere when you tell the beautiful story of how
we met
Honestly when you speak of me, tell them how selfish I was and
how you really wish you could forget

Uhlamurile Mabunda

Just My Day

I missed you today, it killed me that I couldn't tell you
But in my soul, I wished I still kissed you each day
I look at pictures of you and hear the little words you'd say
Thinking how to hold and hug you would really go a long way
Nothing could express the pain in this feeling, not even an essay
It's impossible to be with you, but, I missed you today.

What Do I Miss?

I miss the idea of you, not you, just what I thought of you
Because you wanted to talk when I was willing to listen
And I had ideas that we could one day be happy together
A lucid dream that you would one day have my children
Inspired by the concept of endless nights of chatty humour
But I don't miss you, I just miss that about you.

The Side

The one who never has to look at the bills after the thrills
And gets taken on weekends away beyond the hills
Whose tasty body embellishes videos and camera stills
The one who feeds you endlessly when your hunger wills

And will not see wedding rings but beaches in her views
Knows she will never sit next to your mother in the pews
But be seen as the side despite her makeup and its hues
Will sleep alone and empty one day after she is used

In the Moment

Speak words that start a fire and entice her mind
Dim the lights and watch the lumens dance off her attention
Tame her eagerness as she stares in bewilderment of your devotion

Pull her close, hold her by the waist of her desires
Feel the fabric of her urges on your sensuous skin
Slowly undress her fears and teach her to sense unrestricted
Undo her stress and let her body drift into your arms
Carry her and lay her yearnings down in your presence
Let the future you talk about linger on her prurient lips

Move your hands up her dreams and sculpt her hopes
Lightly touch her face and inhale her amorous smiles
Gently stroke the nape of her neck with a soft assurance
Kiss her naval, slowly drop her inhibitions to her feet
Massage the baggage off her back and inner thoughts
Drape her past over your shoulders and suck on her anxieties
Lick every delicious wound she has and enchant her insecurities
Let your tongue escort her through your hallucination of her

Hold her up against a wall over your intentions of her
Trace her alluring contours into the stencil of your fantasy
Decadently make love to her desires of being your world
Let each stroke you incite paint a life she longs to want
Reach for the universe, take her hand and speak to her

Melancholy

*(n) a deep feeling of sadness that lasts for a
long time and often cannot be explained.*

BookFive

"
so even though we may
experience pain along the way
"

Uhlamurile Mabunda

The Father's Struggle

Sacrifice may have scared his heart,
But failure could not tear him apart,
Not even when success had to depart,
Nor obligation was in character to play its part
His every breath was life right from the start,
The world was bound to make room for his portrait,
A generational landscape of great importance.

The offspring that graduated from the womb to gain the world
    whole.
A piece of him in each, commissioned to achieve what he didn't,
To do what he couldn't, life dare it not deny them, it wouldn't …
And though the man cherished life enough to have fathered three,
They were blessed to be his sons, and live on as his testimony.

On such a day, the sons looked to the heavens and cried mercy,
Against their emotions which had settled on "why do you curse
    me?"
For the old man's death had caused their hearts to bleed
And like eaglets out the nest, tears they all had to cede …
And though their case they might want to plead, it just couldn't be
Because not everything in life was theirs to keep, despite being
    free.

A Cut of Grief

Astonishment is all I had when I heard. I felt completely covered in a heavy sorrow-lined coat, weighing on my very heart and weaving hurt into every thread. I didn't accept it, I kept trying to rub out the pain and wipe it with smiles and all I did was press them in.

Full-figured memories walking in pinstriped moments, while pins strike my heart with every passing moment. I wondered how long I would keep it clean and neatly on display. I wonder how I would hold back tears at the seams and not have them rip apart this plus-sized hope.

Tailored brokenness and questions of why scars are used to cover so little of what we are meant to show. I'm relentlessly draped in all this despondent linen and I feel burdened. The texture of the misery has me in tears and I ask God questions whose answers I cannot touch. I remember your life every day, and I will tell your descendants about you one day.

Walking out, you took your turns ten years apart, I kept telling myself that it was not the right cut but it could be made the impeccable fit. I took it off because observing it was acceptable enough. And all you've left me with I've ironed and neatly packed away – I don't wear grief well.

If Words Meant a Thing

In me I see what you saw
So, let me say what I did not show
Where I would guide you to, I did not know
In turn my role with you I was never sure
Let me write this out so my heart will pour

I failed to lead you and that I'll admit
The coward in me tried to lie and maybe fake it
Faithful to my first promise, so truth I had to submit
Reluctantly plundered your passions and left as a bandit
I struggled to find a version of us to which I'd commit

And I know my rhyme schemes will not dry your teary face
Maybe my lousy apology leaves us someday in a better place
In itself an elaborate scheme to pacify the pain
If words meant a thing, I'd say I'm sorry I couldn't let love reign

Missing Child

I sat in the dark feeling things I never have
Thinking you could have been my baby girl
Imagined the elation, I could have had
In a future where you existed and lived

Cold reality in missing you, unborn as you are
I can't say were – your absence is present now
I may not hold you but carry your essence now
My spirit never really made peace losing you
I tremor that I almost was a father to you
Tears fell as I wrote this silent letter for you

Despite never meeting you dear child
And feeling orphaned by my own offspring's end
I sometimes wake up to see if it's you by my side

Phases

Dear Ex
I loved you once
I haven't felt that since
But I can't go through that again
I loved you my way and you rejected me anyway
It wasn't love if it wasn't exclusively your way
I tell myself it's okay as I walk away
Feel no more pain for today
I'll try again another day

Us?

We left us

Abandoned behind the shrine
I know my wick was fine
My touch was of the fire kind
And it was only a subject of time
Until you had all that was mine
Our affection was unconfined

We let us wither and die!
Look, your big eyes work just fine
But it's your soul that was blind
Never thought we'd cross that line
My chest had a warm home sign
But it was my heart that was cold

We left us

Uhlamurile Mabunda

The Sight of Pain

I see the joy, weeping at the sight of the imaginary rose garden,
    tarnished, bruised and battered, the
Untouched rose confused by all the pain is all that mattered.
I see the future in your past, it will be told by the tears you have
    shed for me, desertion-plated thorns and
The concrete soil keeping it stemmed to the ground is all that we
    see.
I see the light fighting with your darkness, my days are numbered,
    it's bound to hunt me down and make a mockery of my
    existence, once more humbled.
I've seen it all before, smiled the teary-eyed blind man, and I'll
    feel it all again.

Thespians and Companions

It hurt to learn what you really thought of me on the side
Self-importance only believed it could give out help
I thought your intelligence was inspired and thoughts allied
But you smiled at friends, spoke about their flaws in tongues so
    snide
I guess you see friends a different way when their use is expired

Your false conclusions taught me a valuable lesson
Struggled to listen to anyone you thought was the lesser
Sanctimoniously speaking, believing you were the better
Since the education said on a paper that you were a master
Should have also told you that your opinion wouldn't matter

Truth is I'm not innocent either, my judgement is thinly veiled
My flaws are plenty, inscribed on my spirit in braille
I hid my fears in belief, they left my spirit weak and frail
I've been through enough to learn that I'm not afraid to fail
Hard to tell apart thespian from companion and when you set sail

I still don't know which you were even while I tell this tale

What Am I to You?

I do not knock, I do not ask, I won't even let you finish a task
I am the world hide-and-never-seek champion, in your peril I bask
My silence starts speaking to you and your ghosts smile for the
    people

Reality becomes an enemy in a world where fiction is a comforting
    idol
And the mob in universal rhymes buries any disturbance caused
    by reason
My trance is filled with lust and electroplated with peace if only
    for a season
With time I'll break you down away from people keeping just
    enough for treason
I will abuse you and thou shall learn to make excuse for me and
    my legion

Your beautiful fake smile will surely suppress any suspicion of this lesion

My inner clown, hidden frowns and resilient appearance will gag every call of distress

I cast illusions so you sleep and lie there motionless and make it feel like progress

Your outcry is never out loud but betrays the soul it holds captive with limbs and actions

If you look closely, your own body behaves in actions that mimic those of factions

Yesterday's loss will still seem better than today because you survived me then

I am anxious to have you answer the question I will ask, what am I to you?

Elation

(n) a feeling of great happiness and
excitement; exultant gladness.

BookSix

"

we persevere because our lives
and happiness depend on it

"

Allow Me To

Walk around with a sinister smile like I know where the next
foot goes,
Say it with a tranquil voice like I know where the next word
blows,
Let my fingers dance in hope they show what the soul knows,
Learn to live because I know that's just how love grows,
Cherish another so I can say a lover's heart glows,
Because life is too short and so is this poem.

Little People

I sometimes look at the joy my presence brings you and wonder
    why I am not always that happy
I look at all the things you appreciate and I find trivial and I realise
    that I've let my happy grow naggy

You have no demands of me except that I play with you
You cry when I leave you and smile when I see you

When I have a son and a daughter, I'll tell them about the child
    who brought me laughter
Who taught me that a child's dreams need to be looked after

You may be little and marble eyed, but you carry the biggest love
    inside
I wish I could bottle your innocence every time you fall asleep by
    my side

You lent me time that I didn't know how to spend, every minute
    was something warm and kind of fuzzy
I understand why my time meant everything to you, looking back
    at it now it means the world to me

You have loved me and I did not know you called me daddy
I hope I'll visit soon, and if it's all right with you, I will call you
    my baby

Trumpets to Heaven

I can only imagine him seated at the table teaching the angels and ancestors mastery of the trumpet's growl, infusing it magically with his own howl, the paradox of the one that sat with spiritual beings imparting soul.

Majestic half notes of Miles and Luis bouncing coloured hues on the register, reserving a place for you right in the middle with a seat at the table of blues and an African-forged trumpet engraved with the inscription just for Hugh.

The sun set and cast a horn-shaped shadow immortalised in brass, sounding to the masses that the jazz procession is in session, blowing trumpets in heaven.

Sweet Art

Your soul tastes like cinnamon tart!
So decadently addictive to the heart
Like a hundred cakes of art
Or a unicorn pulling pudding karts
Riding fudge rainbows to the mart
Skin kissing raindrops made from sweethearts

Those jelly eyes gaze and dart
At sour trifles, easy to thwart

Caramel smiles are just the start
When honey praises your lips depart
And candy laughter the daily stalwart
Your body of chocolate is counterpart

Steaming Hot

I liked to show up at your door
Like I needed you just a little more
Easily play wrestle you to the floor
Adorn compliments on what you wore
Moving along a cloth-painted corridor
Yet, we never made it to the bedroom door

Free

Sometimes it will take your wallet being empty
To pay the price for your heart to be happy

Poiesis

This is an ode to prose and prologues
Monologues and violent acrostics
Lyrics that outstrip elaborate limericks
Epics that travel to hearts in couplets

Sonnets that refrain from pretty ballads
Melodies chanting freedom for verses
Like rhyming similes in haiku rhetoric
Asserting assonance and alliteration in

Imagery of ironic metaphors masking
Stanzas that poeticise the narrative

"We need to respect and love our women wholeheartedly so that we unite and collectively take back our power as a people and formulate thoughts that lead us to a better sense of self. Actively nurture and grow fruitful and loving relationships, so even though we may experience pain along the way, we persevere because our lives and happiness depend on it."

Gratitude

Thank you for reading my book.

I hope it has given to you as much emotion reading it as I poured into writing it.

– Uhlamurile Mabunda

Notes

Notes

Notes

Notes

Notes

Notes